Genre Historical Fiction

Essential Question
How do people show inner strength?

Making Some NEWS

BY TERRY MILLER SHANNON
ILLUSTRATED BY ANDREW BURDAN

CHAPTER 1

THE LETTER

"Ezekiel Freeman!" Teacher shouted.

Zeke quickly dropped the end of Flossie's pigtail. He had been holding it over the pot of ink on his desk.

"What do you think you're doing, young man?" Teacher asked sharply.

There was nothing Zeke could say. He could tell her that dipping Flossie's braid in ink was **retaliation** because earlier that day, Flossie had tied his shoelaces together. But Teacher wouldn't believe him.

Zeke wasn't really sorry, but he tried to sound **sincere** and honest as he apologized to Flossie. It was hard to ignore the laughter dancing in her bright eyes.

"Ezekiel Freeman, I don't know what to do with you," Teacher said with a sigh.

Many people said hello to Zeke as he walked home after school. In a small town like Weeksville, everybody knew everyone else.

Zeke almost stopped at the newspaper office to say howdy to his mother, but then he remembered that Ma had stayed home from work because she was sick. He thought of how pale and tired she had looked that morning.

"Go find Miss Jenny and ask her to stop by later today," Ma had said. "I'll ask her to help me write a letter to your grandma."

Zeke paused on the front **stoop** when he reached his house. He could hear two people talking inside. One of them was Miss Jenny's daughter—Flossie! Her mother must have sent her to help Ma write the letter to Grandma.

The boy looked over his shoulder since he didn't want to be caught **eavesdropping**.

Ma said, "Write this: 'You know, Mama, I can't really count on Zeke.'" Zeke felt a cold pit in his stomach. He stopped breathing.

Ma continued, "Zeke is funny and he tells good stories, but he's far from becoming a man."

Zeke didn't want to hear more, so he turned and ran away.

STOP AND CHECK

How does Zeke hear what his mother thinks of him?

CHAPTER 2

HELP NEEDED

The next morning, Zeke couldn't stop thinking about what his mother had said. He still heard her voice saying, "He's far from becoming a man."

Zeke rolled out of bed, put on his dungarees and a shirt, and tiptoed down the hall and peeked into his mother's dark room.

Zeke stepped up to Ma's bed and touched her hand. It was as hot as the stove. "I should get the doctor," he said, feeling worried.

"No," she whispered, "we can't pay him."

The son knew that he couldn't obey his mother this time. **Undaunted** by her words, he ran to Doc's home.

"Your mama is very sick," Doc Lincoln said after he had examined her. "She must stay in bed until she is stronger. And she won't be able to work for a long time."

Zeke promised that he would help his mother. He walked the doctor to the door and then came back with a glass of cool water for Ma.

Looking deep into Zeke's eyes, Ma said, "You need to find a job, Ezekiel. We don't have enough money to pay the doctor or buy food."

"Come on, Ma," Zeke said. "I'll be so busy taking care of you I won't have time to work."

She was too tired to smile. "I'm sorry, son, but we need money for food," she said seriously.

Just then Zeke heard Miss Jenny calling, "I've brought you custard and biscuits. They're good enough to make you rise up off your bed!"

Miss Jenny was always full of energy. She **bustled** into the room, followed by Flossie.

STOP AND CHECK

Why does Zeke's mother want him to get a job?

As soon as Zeke saw Flossie, he remembered what Ma had said about him. But Flossie was looking at Ma's face, not thinking about Zeke.

"You and Zeke go to school now," Miss Jenny said to Flossie. "Zeke, don't worry about your mama. I'll take good care of her, and soon she'll be as strong as a mule."

Day after day, Miss Jenny and the other women from the neighborhood cooked and cleaned for Zeke and his mother.

One evening Ma called Zeke to her room. "You need to find work, son," she said.

Zeke jerked away. Why didn't his mother understand? He was not **disposed** to working.

"We're doing fine, Ma," he said with a smile. "We just had Miss Bertha's chicken soup!"

But she was serious. "No, son," she said. "We need to have our own money."

The next day, Zeke walked slowly home from school. When he **strolled** past the newspaper office, Ma's boss, Mr. Jackson, opened the door and asked Zeke to come in to talk.

Zeke stepped into the office and took a deep breath. The office didn't smell as fresh as usual since Ma hadn't been there to clean it.

"We miss having your mama in the office," Mr. Jackson said. "But I'm going to keep her job for her until she's well enough to come back."

"Thank you, sir," Zeke said.

Mr. Jackson polished his glasses with a red handkerchief. "I have an idea, Zeke," he said. "This office is getting mighty dirty without the **rigors** of your mama's cleaning."

Zeke looked around and saw that the office did look pretty grimy. The furniture was dusty, and the floor needed to be swept.

"It would really help us if you worked here after school," Mr. Jackson said. "I'd pay you the same that I pay your mama."

Zeke was disappointed—his heart sank down to his boots. After school, all he had to do was check on his mother and then he played ball until he came home to a meal cooked by a neighbor.

But he remembered Ma's words: "I can't really count on Zeke." He wanted to prove her wrong.

"I'd be honored, sir," he said.

STOP AND CHECK

Why does Mr. Jackson offer Zeke a job?

CHAPTER 3

STORYTELLER

Zeke knew he should be grateful for the job. Instead, he was annoyed and **resented** giving up his free time. Ma was happy that he was working and proud of his **fortitude**. But he still grumbled.

Even though Zeke hated his job, he liked Mr. Jackson. The boy enjoyed telling him jokes and stories. His boss had a rich, warm laugh, and he always laughed long and hard at Zeke's tales.

Zeke began to pay special attention to what people said and did because he wanted more stories to tell his employer.

Mr. Jackson roared with laughter whenever Zeke told a story about Flossie. This time, he told him about the day she put cold custard in his desk.

"I screamed when I put my finger in it," Zeke admitted. "Then she turned around, trying to look innocent, and asked what was wrong."

"That does it, Zeke," Mr. Jackson said, wiping his eyes. He suddenly looked very serious.

Zeke thought Mr. Jackson was angry. He started sweeping **vigorously**, pushing the broom quickly and strongly. "I'm sorry, Mr. Jackson," he said. "I know I let my tongue wag too much."

His boss told Zeke to put the broom away. Zeke's shoulders slumped. If he lost his job, it would prove that Ma had been right about him.

"I'll try harder, Mr. Jackson, sir," he **pleaded**. "I'm begging you to please let me stay."

Surprised, Mr. Jackson laughed. “Zeke, I’m not letting you go. You have no talent for cleaning, but you’re very good at telling stories.”

“I don’t understand, sir,” the boy said.

“I have big plans for you, Ezekiel Freeman. I want you to interview people and write down their stories. If the stories are good enough, I’ll give you a job as a reporter and raise your pay.”

Zeke was shaking his head before Mr. Jackson finished speaking. He could think of an **infinite** number of reasons why he did not want the job. The most important reason was that it would be too much work. Pushing a broom around was bad enough, but writing stories would be even harder.

"Thank you kindly, Mr. Jackson, sir," Zeke said, "but I'd rather keep cleaning until Ma can work. She's feeling better now. She'll be back any day!"

"You're not getting off that easily," Mr. Jackson said, smiling. He walked around his desk to hand Zeke a piece of paper and a pencil. "Your first job is to interview Mr. Jacob Washington. You can write the story of how he became our town blacksmith."

Zeke opened his mouth to say he was quitting, but then he remembered how proud Ma was of his job. And he knew they needed the money. He did not want to write stories for Mr. Jackson, but he felt like he didn't have a choice.

Zeke felt very nervous as he walked up to Mr. Washington's blacksmith shop. His voice squeaked as he asked his first question, but the boy calmed down when Mr. Washington began talking about how he became a blacksmith. The story caught Zeke like a fish on a line.

Zeke smiled as he walked back to the newspaper office, clutching his pages of notes. Maybe Mr. Jackson was right. He loved hearing stories and telling them, too. In his new job as a reporter, he'd have the chance to do both.

He couldn't wait to tell his mother about his job, but she had news for him, too. As soon as Zeke got home, she told him, "Doc Lincoln said I can go back to work! Now you can quit working and play ball with your friends after school."

Zeke didn't even pause to think. "I can't quit now, Ma," he said. "I have big news!"

STOP AND CHECK

Why does Zeke decide to write stories for Mr. Jackson?

Respond to Reading

Summarize

Use key events from *Making Some News* to summarize the story. Your graphic organizer may help you.

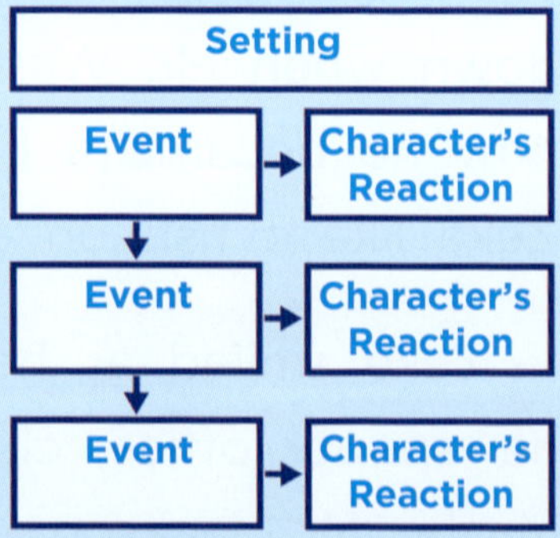

Text Evidence

1. Why does Zeke agree to clean for Mr. Jackson? **CAUSE AND EFFECT**

2. Find the word *grimy* on page 10. What clues help you to understand the word's meaning? **VOCABULARY**

3. Reread Chapter 4. Write about the events that lead to Zeke becoming a reporter for Mr. Jackson. Why does Zeke want to keep working after Ma says he can quit? **WRITE ABOUT READING**

Genre Folktale

Compare Texts

Read about a boy and his mother who find the courage to defeat a monster.

WILEY Outwits the Hairy Guy

One day Wiley's mother asked him to gather firewood in the forest. Wiley was afraid because he'd heard about the Hairy Guy who lived there. His mother told him to take his dog, Spot, with him. The monster was terrified of dogs.

Wiley was gathering branches when he saw the huge, scary-looking beast stomping toward him. Just then, Spot ran off after a squirrel.

Wiley noticed that the Hairy Guy had giant chicken feet. The boy quickly climbed a tree. No one could scale a trunk with chicken feet!

"Come down from there!" the ugly giant yelled.

"No way!" Wiley responded.

The Hairy Guy started chopping down Wiley's tree! The boy held on tightly as the tree began to shake. Just then, Spot saw the Hairy Guy and started barking. The monster ran away as fast as his chicken feet could carry him.

The next day, Wiley's mother wanted more firewood, so he took a deep breath and returned to the forest.

Once again, the Hairy Guy found Wiley. And once again, Wiley climbed a tree. The Hairy Guy laughed and began chopping down the tree.

But Spot came looking for Wiley. When the big beast saw the dog, he got scared and ran away into the dark forest.

On his way home, Wiley had a great idea. He couldn't wait to tell his mother.

Illustration: Bob Brugger

That night, Wiley and his mother laid Spot in Wiley's bed and covered him with a blanket. Then Wiley's mother went outside and yelled, "Hairy Guy, I want to make a deal!"

The big monster shouted from the forest, "What kind of deal?"

Wiley's mother yelled back, "If I give you the little one sleeping in Wiley's bed, will you promise to go away forever?"

The Hairy Guy paused for a long moment, then he said, "Yes, I promise."

Wiley's mother led the beast up to Wiley's room. The Hairy Guy stomped over to the bed and pulled back the blanket.

Spot growled louder than he'd ever growled before. And the scared giant ran away faster than ever. And he kept his promise. Wiley and his mother never saw the Hairy Guy again.

Make Connections

What helps Wiley and his mother face the Hairy Guy? **ESSENTIAL QUESTION**

Compare how Zeke and Wiley find ways to do something they didn't believe they were able to do. **TEXT TO TEXT**

Focus on

Literary Elements

Imagery Imagery is language that describes how something looks, sounds, smells, feels, or tastes. Writers use imagery to help describe the settings, events, places, and characters in stories.

Read and Find The author writes that Wiley saw "the huge, scary-looking beast stomping toward him." The words the author uses help readers to picture, or imagine, the beast Hairy Guy. *Huge* and *scary* show what the Hairy Guy looks like. *Stomping* shows how he moves.

Your Turn

Work with a partner. Look for examples of imagery in *Making Some News*.

Find a description of a character or place. Which words help you to imagine how the character or place looks, sounds, or smells?

Find a word that helps you picture how a character speaks or moves. What does this show about the character?